Walk

Destiny

---

living in His increase

Compiled by Kathleen D. Mailer

To Jen
you have been a wonderful blessing to me, I have learned so much from you about being my true self and not following in what I feel are ways others will accept me: I truly love your giving heart. Love and Hugs
BW

Copyright © 2016

ISBN 978-1-897054-82-6

Published by: Aurora Publishing – a Division of: Doing Business God's Way International Inc.

Walking in Your Destiny, Living in His Increase
Compiled by Kathleen D. Mailer

The publisher gratefully acknowledges the many publishers and individuals who granted our *Walking in Your Destiny* team the permission to reprint the cited material.

DISCLAIMER: Each author is writing from her own viewpoint and it does not necessarily reflect the viewpoint of the publisher, compiler, editor, and other members of the team. It is written to inspire, motivate, and activate each heart that reads it. The reader cannot hold the publisher, compiler, editor, or any other members of the team accountable for any outcomes or conclusions they come to as they read.

Walking in Your Destiny
living in HIS increase

Dedication

This book is dedicated to the amazing people who came to the "A Book Is Never A Book Boot Camp" in 2016.

I am so proud of you! It has been such a complete pleasure to watch this little gem unfold as you let the life of Jesus flow through you and onto these pages. May this book help you go to the next level in your life, your business, and your ministry!

Walking in Your Destiny living in HIS increase

Table of Contents

Acknowledgements i

Introduction v

The Year of Increase
Kathleen D. Mailer 1

My Gift
Sari Buhler 19

Calming the Waves
Bev Burton 27

Woman of God – My Gifts, His Gifts
Naomi (Noni) Deutekom 35

Bring Back The Music
Jennifer Johnson 43

Two Hearts Two Souls
Suzanne D Jubb 51

My Story Has Changed!
Margie McIntyre 61

Anchovies, Spaghetti Squash, and a
Chocolate Bar
Daniela Peregrina 71

A Strong Tower
Cheryl Regier 83

Birth of BACC (Bibles at Cost Canada)
Karen Skelton 95

Increase – God's Step-By-Step Plan
Dannielle Somerville 105

The Jesus I Never Knew
Deborah Hoback Veuger 113

God, What is YOUR Purpose for Me?
Ruth Yesmaniski 121

Walking in Your Destiny
living in HIS increase

Acknowledgements

I would personally like to thank our wonderful team that worked behind the scenes to help make the Book Boot Camp unique, special, and meaningful.

Special thanks go to Dan Mailer who is always present, always pulling together every last detail, and always a pillar of strength in our events. Without your covering, these events would never have the impact they are meant to have.

To Cheryl Regier and Ruth Yesmaniski who graciously gifted us with their editing services for the purpose of this project, I thank you. Your heart to serve the Lord is inspirational. I know you were "pressed in" for the time frame (getting the book written, edited, and published in less than 7 days makes it a monumental challenge). You took the challenge, and you delivered. Thank you.

Thank you to Dannielle Somerville for her contribution to making the Boot Camp a success. Having you work alongside of me has truly been one of my greatest joys in life. Not only is it fun to mentor you through the steps of starting your own business ministry, Proverbs 31 Events, but watching you blossom into the essence of a Proverb 31 Woman yourself is more than I could have imagined. I am so very proud to be your Mom! You are a vital part of our business ministry team. Together, we are stronger. This makes us more able to do the work of our Father.

This would not be complete if I didn't acknowledge one of the most AMAZING graduating classes of the Book Boot Camp. This year was beyond my wildest imagination. Even with the challenges many of our students faced to get to the event, you came and conquered. It is truly my pleasure and honor to watch each star rise to new heights. You are like satellites sent out from the HUB of Messenger Central! I love it! Your inevitable success is evident within the pages of this treasure book.

Praise you, Lord Jesus, for giving us life and giving it in abundance! My gratitude is beyond words. I pray that my life will somehow be worship to you.

Holy Spirit, let every word and every page in this book breathe the breath of Christ. I pray that the words and stories within not only inspire others to take purposed action, but also give them courage to walk in their own faith walk – marching forward in their destiny.

Father in Heaven, only You could bring a family together and have the gathering like this so filled with joy and healing.

I love you!

Kathleen D. Mailer

Walking in Your Destiny
living in HIS increase

Introduction

Here I am, once again, pinching myself. I can hardly believe all of this – watching God work through us and our partners – is real.

Residing in the middle of God's grace is truly living the blessed life.

Storms can come: uncomfortable circumstances can try and push you down; you may get sick, diagnosed with something that usually kills and destroys; or maybe a loved one may die, leaving you wondering why and feeling a little lost.

The one thing that remains greater than all of these things is that His love never fails. It never gives up and is a never ending well of life-giving water.

I have learned to walk in the wake of the Holy Spirit. I am being lifted on wings like eagles, soaring above all things. God's mercies are new every morning, and they endure forever.

I have noticed something else that holds a wealth of truth. The Lord reminds me of this even now. With every new trial we face, He gives us the ability to grow, mature, and move past it. As a result, He gives us increase. It is an increase in favour, health, influence, relationships, gifts, finances, grace, and wisdom.

This has been very evident even since the last **'A Book is Never a Book'** Boot Camp.

That is why the theme for this year's *Walking in Your Destiny Book* is *living in His increase*. Let me give you a little background so you will know where I am coming from.

Like last year, this year's Boot Camp has grown exponentially in its branding message.

God has INCREASED our ability to keep our marketing message simple, give more value, and create positioning so that others can expand a platform for their purpose.

As a matter of fact, this is the precise reason we do the Boot Camp. We want to help you take your message to the masses in a clear and simple way. Your flock is waiting for you to help them understand clearly what God has for them. They want to be equipped, encouraged, and educated. Am I right?

We also know that God has called you to not only share your message, but to build a BUSINESS MINISTRY. Yes! He WANTS you to make money doing it. Why?

Well... several reasons come to mind:

> *"God gives us a business so we can go out and DO God's business."*

This simply means you are designed to create money to fund Kingdom purposes (which includes increase in your household).

God Himself gives you the power to create wealth, and so many seem to be confused by this. Please don't be confused. It is the will of God that you live an abundant life. If it wasn't His will, He would have said so.

"Your history is really HIS-story!"

You are called to steward this gift you call life for the purposes and plans of God.

"There is POWER in your testimony!"

You are chosen by God to use your testimony to help others see hope. If you have decided that you don't want to write that book or share your story, that choice is between you and God. However, I respectfully will say this: In order for you to fully walk in your destiny, **sharing the Good News of Christ is a foundational part.**

But you are the ones chosen by God, chosen for the high calling of priestly work, chosen to be a holy people, God's instruments to do His work and speak out for Him, tell others of the night-and-day difference He made for you – from nothing to something, from rejected to accepted. 1 Peter 2:9 (MSG)

In the next chapter, I will share the powerful prophetic word that God gave me at the start of this year. It was not just for me. It is for you, too, as well as for those you influence. INCREASE IS HERE!

Since last year, we have seen increase in very tangible ways. Here are a few, as it pertains to our 'partners'. (This is what we call our family of authors. You bring your gifts, talents, and abilities, and we will bring ours. Together, we will give God the glory!)

www.ChristianAuthorsGetPaid.com

This new brand has now become the HUB of everything we do. It is just in its infancy right now, but it is designed to be the center through which we can help Christian authors grow and expand in every area of life.

We will bring teachings, programs, monthly coaching, boot camps, training sessions, etc.

These are designed to help you steward your story and WRITE your book. In addition, you will learn how to position it into a movie platform, to speak for success, to write it into a song, and to package it to bring monthly income and increase.

We will also teach you to PUBLISH each of those things with simplicity and ease. You do have to know the ins and outs of the publishing process in every one of those areas.

The teaching will be made complete because of the MARKETING arm we are working on. Marketing is simply adding value to your readers, students, or audience. It is something that must be an ongoing thing for all of us in order to fulfill the call on our life.

We are a community creating a movement for God. We want to work 'together' to help one another succeed!

Wait for it! There is more!

Walking In Your Destiny Series

This little book has been one of the highlights in our Boot Camp in the last 2 years.

It is a real life example of how we use what we teach to create a platform to help our students become all who God has called them to be.

In the Boot Camp, we not only help you find your message, your title, and the complete outline for your own book, we use the same formula to craft chapters in this series so that you can leave the Boot Camp a PUBLISHED AUTHOR!

This book may help you open doors to more speaking engagements, give you credibility in your business or current ministry, create an extra stream of income (buy it wholesale and sell retail), give you confidence to move forward in your own walk with Christ, and so much more!

Powerful FREE Trainings

Throughout the year, all over the world, we are providing **free trainings** designed to get you started.

Things like:

- 7 Lies the Devil Dishes Out to Stop You from WRITING that BOOK!

- 7 Ways To Use Your Knowledge to CREATE WEALTH Now!

- The Simplicity Formula™ – A Multiple Platform Tool (Blogs, Social Media, Articles, and Books) that will help you WRITE it RIGHT!

You can stay connected with us through:

FB: KathleenD.Mailer (Public Figure)
Twitter: @KathleenMailer
LinkedIn: Kathleen Mailer
www.KathleenMailer.com
www.ChristianAuthorsGetPaid.com
www.ABookIsNeverABook.com
www.TodaysBusinesswomanMagazine.com

Needless to say, I can't wait until next year to see what God has in store for all of us who love Him. Amen? I am ready for even more increase. Are you?

I pray that you will enjoy this book and its powerful message. I also pray that you take inspired action today – to start walking in your powerful destiny!

We would love to hear from you!

Feel free to email our head office:
AuroraPublishing@shaw.ca

Let's move on.........

In Jesus' precious name,

With love, Kathleen

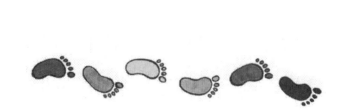

Walking in Your Destiny living in HIS increase

The Year of Increase

Kathleen D. Mailer

January 2016,

ARE YOU READY?

As the Lord spoke to me, I give to you. May it bless you, make you tremble in fear, and stand in awe – as it did me. May it spur you into taking action, into creating a vision for your life with God in the midst, to live out of the Word, and encourage you to go deeper with our LORD, more than you have ever been before.

Please also note: I did not capitalize satan's name on purpose. Why? Because a long time ago, I decided he is nothing but a little 's'. He doesn't deserve any respect or honour. This was done in 'free flow' through worship and praise. Therefore, it is a different format than the writings of this book. Are You Ready?

This year will emerge like a tidal wave. It will be like nothing you have ever seen or heard. Earthquakes, Tsunamis, Volcanoes erupting... all are signs that the time has come and I, the Lord your God, have put into motion what no man can stop. **satan won't be able to get to you, through you, over you, or around you. The ONLY place he can go is under your feet!**

My purposes and plans for your life will come to pass because I have created you for a time such as this.

These 'acts of nature' will be sent as a reminder to the whole world. It is I who is truly in control. While others struggle and strive (the 'you' of your past), you will find **this a season of ease as we enter through the gates of 2016.**

You leave 2015 – a year without limitations – knowing that you have broken through so many of the things that held you hostage. Strongholds and fleshly desires were set down before Me at the base of My throne. You learned how to be obedient, even at the expense of pleasing people.

You remained obedient even when every fiber of your body screamed to submit to your carnal desires and walk away from the hurt and pain – you submitted to Me instead. You laid down your flesh to gain MY heart – and I am well pleased.

This year, a cornucopia of harvest will manifest physically – and so many will find themselves in **INCREASE.** Remind them that **with INCREASE of GOODNESS** comes **INCREASE of RESPONSIBILITY**.

For those that are ready, the dam will burst open – even as they read this and declare:

"I AM READY FOR INCREASE! In Jesus' name!"

As soon as the words are spoken, they will 'feel' different. Things will 'look' different, even though at the moment their circumstances and surroundings are the same. HOLD ON TIGHT to **that 'unseen' change because it is about to become a physical reality very, VERY fast!**

Remember to **INCREASE the SIZE OF YOUR TABLE – not the height of your walls.** As you are blessed, be a blessing. Do not HIDE what I, the Lord God, have done for you. Share it with the entire world. **Give it freely – as you have received it freely.**

For those that ask, I have a **supernatural INCREASE OF FAITH** for you. It will be the same increase the apostles received when they asked Me to teach them how to increase their faith. *(Luke 17:5).* Through this **INCREASE of FAITH,** there will be an **INCREASE of ACTION** taken – moving

4

forward day-by-day, week-by-week, month-by-month – resulting in the **GREATEST year of your life.** *(Hebrews 11)*

Through the **ACTS OF FAITH,** you will **live a life worth living**, with **INCREASED PROTECTION** from the enemy's plans to destroy you. No longer will you live under the demonic influence of negativity and lies. You will know that the cup is always half full, not half empty. You will **STAY IN PEACE** as you move forward on a clear path of "what is my next step?" – **walking in the knowing that God is a God of provision.**

Through the **ACTS OF FAITH,** you will see that I am well pleased. And you will **know that nothing is impossible – for I am a God who cares enough to respond to those who seek Me.**

Through the **ACTS OF FAITH,** you will see clearly **your 'WHY'.** You will see your dream and know your purpose, as Noah did. This will keep you on track. This will show the hurting hearts that a **sharp line is drawn between you and the evil, unbelieving world.** Knowing God's purposes and plan for your life will **inspire those you are called to influence,** gently drawing them closer to Me and helping them understand all of the **LOVE I have** for them. As I open My arms and bring them into My family, **I will be their God, and they will be My people.**

Through the **ACTS OF FAITH,** you will **travel to places that are unknown to you** doing things you have never done before. **You have NEVER had success like this!** Do not fear! Though you will be totally out of your comfort zone, **it will always feel like 'home' because you will find Me in the midst. INCREASED FAVOUR AND GRACE** will become a natural component to your day.

Through the **ACTS OF FAITH,** you will **give birth to the dreams and desires of your heart. Although you thought you would never really see My purposes fully emerge**, you have always been holding onto hope. Hope no more! **A barren womb is no match for MY creative plans, for I am the One who created you.** In this time, I will show you that **I am the one who stands by My promises.**

Through the **ACTS OF FAITH,** I will help you **drop anything in your life** that has become (in your past) more important to you than I am. Addictions, idolatry, attachment to rebellion, pride, arrogance, sickness, people pleasing, complaining, and habits of poverty and lack **can be set down for good this year. As you put Me first in your actions** and **you have faith that I am a God of My 'Word', you will come to know what is true, honest, and pure. All gifts that you have are from Me, who has given them to you.**

Through the **ACTS OF FAITH**, you will **topple kingdoms of darkness**, bring **justice to the world**, be **protected from lions, fires, and sword thrusts. All disadvantages will be turned to advantages** and **you will win** the battles you have been fighting. A time **for INCREASED CELEBRATIONS and FUN** will come as a direct result of the FREEDOM you have found!

And that is not all….

You will have **INCREASE in your FINANCES!** For those who have learned the law of the tithe (10%) – you will now experience an **INCREASE of GIVING.**

For many, they will start by increasing their 'tithe' by 2%, giving 12% unto the Lord of Lords! 10% tithe with go to their church as I have commanded… and 2% as an offering into Kingdom Purposes. I will nudge them daily in their walk as to who I would have them give the 2% to. **Soon, they will find themselves asking Me for more to give – and of course, I won't refuse their request.**

As you choose to participate, I will use you to be My hands and feet to bless others. This physical giving will increase for you this year on a multiplication scale. By the end of the year, you will see an **INCREASE in effortless GIVING** – for some, by 30%; some, 60%; and others, 90% over last year!

This will be shown to you two-fold:

First, a generous spirit will unfold around you. You will be a direct recipient of My generosity through others that I whisper to. This is one way that your personal needs will be met. Many of you will receive gifts of time, money, cars, houses, favour, grace, healing, and opportunities.

PROVISION IS EVERYWHERE.

Yes, even things like clothes, new furniture, and so much more!

Second, you will get to 'partner' with Me – and you will become My hands and feet. Your generous heart is an extension of My heart. **I will give you the seed to sow! ALWAYS and in ALL WAYS**. Keep your ear to My heart in Jesus' name! I want you to walk under a **PROVISIONAL ANNOINT-ING!**

I decree that this will bring about the church of old – when My people **'begged' My servant Paul for the opportunity to give**. The understanding of what true giving is all about will be immeasurable once again. **The cycle of give and receive will be such a delight for you** – and for Me – as **we walk hand-in-hand in a world of those who are hurting**. This truth will be a testimony of Who I Am, and millions will turn from their wicked ways – repent – **and live with Me here on earth and in eternity!**

INCREASE in HEALTH!

This year will be a particularly amazing year of miracles! Of course, I will always bring healing, freedom, and deliverance as I have always done. But this year? This year will bring **an increase of My people wanting to take ACTION** – to bring healing to their bodies through **ACTS OF FAITH.**

Most especially, I will bring the means for them to heal their body, their emotions, and their pain. This is especially true for those who suffer from excess weight issues; it is truly your year to let go of **holding onto the**

ideal of what <u>never</u> works for you. That mindset pushes away My ability to bring healing. This year, you will find the enjoyment of nourishment through My Word (*The Bread of Life*). Many health related symptoms and disorders – like heart problems, blood pressure, weight problems, sleep disorders, energy drains, and depression – will finally be a thing of your past, and you will, in turn, use this healing to reach out to others. You won't be able to help it; it will spill out as a walking testimony of health and healing.

The cure is clear! It is wrapped up, in MY name! Hear Me! I will take you to the way of healing. You and I will do it together. **By your ACTIONS OF FAITH** and by **MY STRIPES,** you are healed in Jesus' name!

INCREASE in RELATIONSHIPS!

Oh yes, this is the year of relationship! Bonds will be strengthened and solidified as you walk through **ACTS OF FAITH** – stepping up and stepping out once again. Vulnerable does not mean abuse cycles start again. It simply means those who are bound in love **will feel a love that surpasses any of their current level of understanding.**

This is a time to **remember to continue to work through the forgiveness issues that hold you in torture and pain.** Where un-forgiveness is released, healing will rush in. It is My promise to you. The more you practice this rule, the faster the blessings can flow. Even if you don't feel like it, just 'act in faith'… and I, the Lord your God, will do the rest.

Old-fashioned letters through the mail, phone calls, and face-to-face dates will once again preside over texts, emails, and social media. It will be a year like no other.

In the past, the devil used My own children to push others away from the love of God and put them into isolation. He did this by influencing them to be judgemental, controlling, thoughtless, religious, jealous, and just plain mean. This year, My children will know that I will love them for them. They will be educated, and they will understand the message of TRUE LOVE. As a result, they will repent from their wicked ways, and I can then use them for MY good and MY glory!

Time for **INCREASED FELLOWSHIP!**

It is a year for the 'BEST FRIEND' to emerge. This will fulfill My plan for My children. For those who have been waiting a very long time for their spouse, **he/she will come, and it will be someone 'unexpected'.**

You have no idea who I have in store for you. **Let go of what you THINK you need or want... and allow Me to show you who I know is 'perfect' for you.**

For those that are married: Your **relationship can only be deepened** this year, as you trust in Me. Forgiveness must live and course through your veins... and you will become more 'one' with Me. **But don't forget that you have friends, sisters, and brothers outside of your marriage.**

I have a good and close friend for you. This is a **friend you can rely on.** Pay close attention and use wisdom. **Lifelong friendships need to mature.** You should 'date' a friend before you commit and jump in with both feet. Be sure **their values, morals and integrity align with My Word and your purpose and platform**. Make sure **you respect each other** and **the work** I have given each of you to do. **Make sure that I am in the center of everything**. Be sure you both hunger for My Word in this relationship because, like every relationship, there will be work involved. **But with commitment, there will be an INCREASE of JOY**. This will then bring you to an **INCREASE of INFLUENCE** through your new relationship!

And finally, My dear one, this year will see a supernatural **INCREASE of INFLEUNCE**.

The time has come when you will be **shown off to the world** as **MY son/daughter!** I want to take you out from behind the bushel and **shine you around the world**.

Together, we will work side-by-side. You will be a walking testimony of how you came from nothing, and I have been made into something in your life. You were rejected;

and now, because you know Me intimately, you are accepted.

This is our year, too, to get to know each other in a greater, more fascinating way.

You will become a **MASTER SHEPHERD** to My flock that I have awaiting you. Try to remember: **It isn't the shepherd that increases the livestock** – it is the **owner of the flocks and fields.**

I have many sheep to add to the land I have given you. Therefore, watch for an **INCREASE OF YOUR FLOCK**.

This year, **diversification is crucial.** No longer will there just be sheep (ahhh...so many without a Shepherd), **but the cattle of a thousand hills are also yours to steward.**

This year, you will find your (My) message being plastered and announced around the world. You will experience a **PLATFORM INCREASE**. The vehicles (books, speaking, programs, products, services, real estate, etc.) will become like a **highly tuned, precision car**, built for the race of life.

You will be in the lead. You are the head and not the tail. Yes, the time has come where **INCREASE IN THE PHYSICAL** will show up, as you have proven yourself **FAITHFUL!**

I love and adore you – My darling daughter/son! I am excited that we are working side-by-side in this wonderful 'FAMILY BUSINESS'!

Beloved, I pray that you hear what I hear – and that you get excited! I pray that **your Faith is deepened, and that you can now ACT in accordance to the FAITH you have been given**.

I pray that any resistance or rebellion to our Lord God and HIS WORD is met by **you taking action** and **letting go of this torture you have been in.**

Get right before God. Repent and ask Him to take the rebellion out of your heart and show you the path to freedom. He **WILL** do so, for He loves you for you – not for what you have done or who you've become. Let Him show you this love. Test Him in this, and you will see a God that is faithful.

You will find a God who WANTS to give you a life filled with abundance, hope, joy, and peace.

If you have any questions or want to share your 'aha' moments, please feel free to connect with us through the Connect Desk: DoingBusinessGodsWay@shaw.ca.

We would be so happy to pray for you – and have you pray for us, as we go through the **YEAR of INCREASE** together.

Be blessed, in Jesus' name! Amen.

Go in Grace and Peace!

Kathleen Mailer

Walking in Your Destiny

living in HIS increase

My Gift

Sari Buhler

After high school, I attended the Peace River Bible Institute in Sexsmith, Alberta, Canada. It was a time of learning and growing in the knowledge of who God was and what He was doing in my life. Coming home after completing my first semester (technically it was the second semester of the school year as I only started in January), God was about to change my life forever. He revealed His presence in my life and anointed me with the gift of teaching in a way I will never forget.

On my first Sunday home, I was excited to go to church and reunite with friends I had not seen in several months. I must admit, I was not thinking about the message I would be listening to. I was more focused on meeting up with my friends and the fun to be had on the soccer field where we gathered every Sunday afternoon. Although my mind was not on church and what I could learn, God's mind was. I will never forget walking into the foyer that day. One of the pastors walked up to me almost immediately, telling me, "Your teacher is sick. Here is the lesson material; you'll have to teach the class".

You know the feeling you get when your heart drops out of your chest? This was the feeling I had at that very moment! I was 19 years old, had never taught a Sunday school class before, and I was supposed to teach my own class full of my friends. My heart was in my stomach and my throat at the same time.

In our church, we always sang for 15 minutes before heading to our various classes.

Panicked, I skipped the singing and went to the area where our class was held to "cram" what lesson planning I could before the class. I remember the relief I felt as I began to read through the material. It was from the book of Romans. The Bible class I had just finished at Bible school the week before had been a study on the book of Romans. I knew this book! I had read it, studied it, and even written a paper on it. God had been preparing me for this very day, not because the class would need a teacher, but because He was about to anoint me with the gift of teaching in a way that would leave no doubt in my heart or mind that this was from Him.

As I began to teach, it was like I was in two places at the same time. Words were flowing out of my mouth and teaching the lesson, even while I carried on a distinct conversation with the Lord inside my head. I knew and recognized that the Holy Spirit was anointing me with His gift of teaching. The words I spoke were His, not mine. He promised me that day that He would always give me His words if I would be obedient and teach His Word – the Bible – to those He sat before me.

I had entered church that day focused on the here and now. I left with a whole new perspective on my life, humbled and in awe of what God had just done in me. It was just as Paul had said, *and we know that in all things God works for the good of those who love Him, who have been called according to His purpose.* (Romans 8:28, NIV) That day, God called me to teach His Word. He had everything worked out; all I had to do was reach out, take that material for the Sunday school lesson, and let Him do the rest.

I knew that I had a responsibility, not only to use my gift, but also to take every opportunity to learn about and study His Word. If I was going to teach His words to others, I would need to *know* Him so that my words would be a reflection of Him, thus leading them into a deeper relationship with Him and not leading them astray. I also realized this was a gift not to be taken lightly. *Not many of you should presume to be teachers, my brothers, because you know that we who teach will be judged more strictly.* (James 3:1, NIV Study Bible)

Finishing Bible school, reading and studying His Word, researching and learning from others…this all became vital to me. *May the words of my mouth and the meditation of my heart be pleasing in your sight, O Lord, my Rock and my Redeemer.* (Psalm 19:14, NIV Study Bible) He called me to teach, and I wanted to please Him.

That Sunday many years ago began a journey of faith and trust. God opened doors for me to teach a variety of Sunday school classes, both children's and adults, as well as Bible study groups. He also provided opportunities to speak to women's groups and youth groups. Through it all, He kept His promise, providing the words that He wanted spoken.

Although God always kept *His* promise, I was not always faithful. There were times when I taught what I thought was important, teaching out of my own agenda. This always fell flat, and it was easy to see and feel the difference between speaking my words and speaking His.

In learning to be faithful and obedient, I had to listen and tune into God's voice. I experienced times when I had studied and prepared for a class all week long, only to have Him wake me up in the middle of the night to give me a new lesson with new words to share with my students. Whether I worked on a lesson for a week or an hour, I discovered that I could always trust Him to give me the words and wisdom I would need for the teaching opportunities He would lead me to and the people He would place before me.

Over the years, God has taught me many things, as I have been faithful to use the gift of teaching. Of these lessons, three stand out:

1. *God does not put us in situations we are unable to handle.* Sometimes it feels this way, but we often see in hindsight how He was preparing us for that specific time. He loves us and wants the best for us, as we are shown in Jeremiah 29:11 – *"For I know the plans I have for you," declares the Lord, "plans to prosper you and not to harm you…"* (NIV)

2. *When we use the gift or gifts He has given us, He uses them to further His kingdom.* I know He will give me the exact words I need to share with others when I need them. He has never let me down, and it does not matter how unsure or nervous I am. When I open my mouth and I am teaching from His will, I am filled with peace, and His words flow out.

3. *He gives His gifts to His children to further His kingdom, but it's up to us to use them.* For me, it can mean sharing with a large or small group or with a single person; it is not about the size of the audience. It is about using His gift in me to lift up others to Him.

In Deuteronomy 29:29, it states that *the secret things belong to the Lord our God, but the things revealed belong to us and to our children forever.* (NIV) I am assured that I do not have to have all the answers. I just have to be obedient. I also recognize that I am human and will fail at times. Nevertheless, I rejoice in *being confident of this, that He who began a good work in* [me] *will carry it on to completion until the day of Christ Jesus.* (Philippians 1:6, NIV)

Through the years, I have watched and rejoiced in how God has used the gift of teaching to increase my knowledge and strengthen my relationship with Him. I look forward to receiving His increase, in whatever form He may choose, as He continues to draw me closer to Him in the years to come.

Sari Buhler *is a published author, wife, and mother. She's taught Sunday school, served as a Sunday school superintendent, and led various Bible study groups, women's prayer breakfasts, and youth groups. Her desire is that God would use her teaching gift to draw others into a closer relationship with Him.*

Walking in Your Destiny living in HIS increase

Calming the Waves

Bev Burton

My pilgrimage with water started when I was an elementary-aged young girl.

We were down at the river where the community would typically gather on a Sunday. Many families who would bring along picnic lunches were always in attendance in search of an afternoon of fun.

On this particular Sunday, the youth were playing a longstanding game in the water where we would join hands in a circle, one person would float up, be released to the outside of the other side of the circle, and then join that side to begin again. My turn came and I went over the arms of those in the circle but instead of being able to stand up as always before, this time there was no river bottom to plant my feet on. As I had never learned to swim, I panicked--my head was under water, I was sinking like a rock and began to inhale water. Thankfully, I was rescued and brought to the river's edge, however, this was the beginning of my "fear journey" with moving water.

From that day forward I would freeze any time I was near moving water. In a boat, even if the water was like glass, I was as rigid as the wood that the boat was made of. Many challenges were presented to me when it rained or the snow melted for living on a farm, in the spring I would find myself needing to cross bodies of water. I was fearful of walking across water that was moving, afflicted with motion sickness and occasionally even falling down.

Leaving home and living in small apartments where there were only showers and no bathtubs brought about great anxiety as I could not stand to have my head under the running water.

As a young adult on holidays with a group, we visited a home that had a pool. One day, I was walking around the edge of the pool watching those in the pool when one of the guys came up behind me and pushed me into the water. Any progress that I had made was now tossed by the wayside, like the strong waves of the sea. Through this experience, my lack of trust issues INCREASED majorly. During this period of time, I did not have God in my life; although I had belief principals that I practised each and every day, I stated to anyone who asked that I did not need God or church.

I lived my early adult life going from one toxic relationship to the next; stuffing, controlling, along with closing myself off from others. I thought that I was in control of things, freezing every time anyone tried to get close, fearing that I would reveal one of my deep dark secrets. I did not allow anyone in, to love or care for me. In fact, because of these fears, I eventually transferred these behaviors that I had developed over my life to my daughter; manifesting in her in the areas of fears, building walls, shame, stuffed feelings, hurts, self-sabotage habits and panic attacks.

Several years later, I was at a business conference that was coming to a close. On that Sunday morning they had a session with worship music, Bible readings, a message, and a call to the stage for anyone wanting to accept Jesus. The first call ended, I continued to sit in my seat. On the second call, one of the ladies from my group went to the front, and upon the third call I got up and walked to stand beside her at the front. What an emotion-filled time this was, the tears flowed like a river as I received Jesus into my heart. This was the beginning of my faith journey which has continued since then primarily by my regular attendance at church to this day.

One day, a few years later, I received a life changing message from God. God spoke to me during a fundraising seminar, letting me know that He wanted me to give up my financial career and to start working on the faith-based areas of my life.

James 1 2-8 *My brethren, count it all joy when you fall into various trials, [3] knowing that the testing of your faith produces patience. [4] But let patience have its perfect work, that you may be perfect and complete, lacking nothing. [5] If any of you lacks wisdom, let him ask of God, who gives to all liberally and without reproach, and it will be given to him. [6] But let him ask in faith, with no doubting, for he who doubts is like a wave of the sea driven and tossed by the wind. [7] For let not that man suppose that he will receive anything from the Lord; [8] he is a double-minded man, unstable in all his ways.*

For the next two years, God and my support team walked with me through the early stages of my recovery journey. God was the Master vinedresser, doing much pruning in order for me to bear the fruit that He planned for me. John 15 *"I am the true vine, and My Father is the vinedresser. [2] Every branch in Me that does not bear fruit He takes away; and every branch that bears fruit He prunes, that it may bear more fruit. [3] You are already clean because of the word which I have spoken to you. [4] Abide in Me, and I in you. As the branch cannot bear fruit of itself, unless it abides in the vine, neither can you, unless you abide in Me. [5] "I am the vine, you are the branches. He who abides in Me, and I in him, bears much fruit; for without Me you can do nothing. [6] If anyone does not abide in Me, he is cast out as a branch and is withered; and they gather them and throw them into the fire, and they are burned. [7] If you abide in Me, and My words abide in you, you will ask what you desire, and it shall be done for you. [8] By this My Father is glorified, that you bear much fruit; so you will be My disciples.*

There have been many times where the waves of doubt, uncertainty, and fear of the unknown have tossed me about, just as a boat on a stormy sea. The more my Faith increases, the calmer the water becomes. Even to this day it takes all my strength in Christ to stand in and by moving water, because of the motion. Relying on the support of Jesus and accepting the encouragement of my trusted family and friends, I can enjoy the water. If it is a beautiful sunny day, I enjoy going for a boat ride. I found great peace while I was on a cruise to Alaska; sitting on the deck, listening to the water, watching the water falls.

Three things I have learned as I reflect on this specific word God has spoken into my life:

1. I am learning to trust in the God of Hope, Love and Trust. <u>Proverbs 3:5-6</u> ***Trust*** *in the Lord with all your heart, And lean not on your own understanding; In all your ways acknowledge Him, And He shall direct your paths.*

2. I find that the more I turn my life over to God and put into action His will and not my will, the more the abundant things He is doing in my life.

3. I am often blown away with the things that happen to me in my life today. There are still times when the waves come in, but they are no longer as high or as strong as they used to be. There are periods of time when I sit and do not move. That is the calm water that is refueling the energy to ride the next set of waves.

Bev Burton *is a coach, leader, and author who works with women that are walking out their healing process. She finds great joy in watching these ladies in their journey of recovery, seeing the light bulbs come on when they identify patterns or habits, both negative and positive.*

Walking in Your Destiny living in HIS increase

Woman of God – My Gifts, His Gifts

Naomi (Noni) Deutekom

I'm not sure where my issues with self-esteem began, but they were reinforced by the era in which I grew up. Any girl who was raised in the sixties and seventies would have struggled with issues of value and worth. Just being a girl set you apart.

I was not unhappy with being a girl. I was unhappy that there were things that seemed to be okay for my brother to do, but were not okay for me to do. Women's roles were being challenged, but I didn't know anything about that at the time. I just saw the inequity and realized that there were fewer opportunities available to me than there were for him. As a result, I learned to see myself as less important than my brother.

My rebellion against that inequity began when I was in elementary school. My father was a teacher, but with five kids to feed and clothe, he often picked up extra jobs. For a while, he worked at the local park office. They had balls and other equipment that could be checked out and a game room that people could use. When I asked if I could come along (my brother was allowed), I was told I was too young. I was eleven months and twenty days younger than my brother was, so for 10 days each year, we were technically the same age. When I had my next birthday, I assumed that I would get to go with Dad. When I asked, the answer was still no, but the reason had changed. I could not go because I was a girl!

I was only seven or eight years old, but I was mad! I decided to run away. I packed my Barbie Doll suitcase and took off down the road. There was a huge vacant lot next to our house, and you could see the end of the block from the yard. When I got there, I had no idea where I was going to go or what I was going to do. My dad came out into the yard and yelled at me to get back to the house. It didn't take much for me to turn around and go home. My dad must have had a change of heart, because he let me go along with him that night and once in a while after that. However, the message had been sent – I was a girl, and that set limits on what I could do.

I found this inequity equally expressed in the church. I remember when I went to Bible School, the first question people asked was: "So, are you going to Bible School to find a husband?" No, I wasn't! I wanted to study the Word of God and grow in Christ. I had always wanted to speak and teach the Word of God. It was my passion. Finding a husband would be a side benefit, but not the reason for going. However, in those days the only ministry options open to women seemed to be to go into missions or to become a pastor's wife. I eventually married, but those ministry opportunities did not become part of my future.

In the years that followed, I taught Sunday school and ladies' Bible studies. I continued to study God's Word on my own, but I always felt that many of my gifts were only acceptable outside the church. I was a leader in many respects, but leadership in the church could only be expressed in either children's or women's ministries, and later on, in worship ministries.

I eventually went back to school and earned a Master of Ministry in Christian Counseling. This opened up ministry for me in a new way. The desire to teach the Word of God and to minister to His people remained foremost in my heart.

I still struggle with these issues from time to time. I have never fit nicely into the role of the "good" Christian wife and mother. However, I have learned to be okay with that. The process of self-acceptance was long and hard.

The conservative Christian society in which I functioned did not seem to have room for all of my gifts, but God did. I learned that living a Christ-focused life could be done in any situation. Ministry was so much bigger than the inside of a church building. God often took me outside the church to encourage and bless others. He also taught me that it was not my job to worry about the outcome.

Through this journey, God brought more understanding to my heart through Psalms 37:

Trust in the Lord, and do good;

Dwell in the land, and feed on His faithfulness.

Delight yourself also in the Lord,

And He shall give you the desires of your heart.

Commit your way to the Lord,

Trust also in Him,

And He shall bring it to pass.

He shall bring forth your righteousness as the light,

And your justice as the noonday.

Psalm 37:3-6 (NKJV)

I truly believe that God has called me to preach and teach His Word. The opportunity to operate in this gifting has presented itself differently at various times in my life. Throughout it all, He has taught me that my responsibility is to trust Him, to commit my way to Him, and to let Him bring it to pass. My job is to dwell in the land in a "bloom where you're planted" way. I am to delight myself *in* Him, allow His gifts to flow in and through me, and He will do the rest.

At one point, God gave me verse 6 in Jeremiah 1 where God calls him to preach. Jeremiah's response is, *"Ah, Lord God! Behold, I cannot speak, for I am a youth."* (NKJV) I came to realize that my response had been, "Behold, I cannot speak, for I am a woman." The Lord let me know that this was not a reasonable excuse. If He had called me, I was empowered and given the authority to speak.

Since then, I have shared the Word as God has lead. Sometimes, God has had me share verbally and sometimes through the witness of the Holy Spirit's work in my life. It is not the avenue through which we preach the Word that is important. What is important is that the message *is* preached.

Recently, God has opened the door for me to begin writing again. Writing and speaking are synonymous for me. The voice is there, whether it is written or spoken. His calling is being fulfilled in my life.

It does not look like I thought it would back in the days of my youth. My gender does not change the message or the call. My circumstances do not change the message or the call. The format and the delivery may change, but not the message or the call. I am to be faithful, to dwell in the land, and to feed on His faithfulness as I operate in the gifting that He has bestowed upon me.

The increase? That's His business, not mine. I commit my way to Him, and He brings it to pass. He gives the increase. He brings forth the fruit. It's not about me, or who I am, or what I want. It's *all* about Him.

Noni currently resides in Dauphin, Manitoba, where she operates a Christian Counseling practice and is active in her local church and community. She loves speaking, teaching, reading, playing the flute, making art, and spending time with friends and family. She believes people are the most important asset in life.

Walking in Your Destiny living in HIS increase

Bring Back The Music

Jennifer Johnson

Some of my earliest childhood memories involve sitting at our family's piano. My parents bought it from my Mom's aunt, and my parents were determined that all three of their daughters would play, and play well. We attended both group and private lessons, and over the years we moved through a number of teachers, of varied ability.

I can't recall whether I actually wanted to play or not, but I do remember trying to fake my Mom out with whether I had practiced properly or not. Unfortunately, she has a musical background, and unless she was not physically present in the house, she could usually tell if I had put in a decent effort, and would send me back to the piano after attempts to slack off and escape to other activities.

My indifference to the instrument changed dramatically in junior high school. I had begun attending a large youth group, where many members sang and played instruments. I was seriously impressed by the accomplished musicians on the Sunday morning worship team at our church. Suddenly, piano playing had relevance and meaning, and after a year or so of having quit lessons, I began taking Royal Conservatory preparation with a different teacher who was also a worship leader. My desire to improve enough to play and sing on our youth worship team grew.

I always knew my Mom had grown up in a musically rich environment, with an older brother who eventually earned a Master's Degree in music, aunts and uncles who sang and played instruments, and herself a beautiful soprano soloist in the small-town Saskatchewan churches they attended. However, I didn't understand her longing for her own children to not only excel musically, but to use it in worship. During this period, Mom shared a prayer that bubbled up from her heart – "God, please bring back the music!" I was just starting to sing in groups, and struggled with hearing myself and staying on key. I was also far behind some of the more accomplished musicians who, though they were of a similar age, were far advanced in their performance and singing abilities. In a large church, this is often the case.

Leaving home was the catalyst God used for refining me as a musician, and eventually directing me into worship leadership. Small town churches pounce on newcomers who can play the piano, even just a little! Over many years, these invaluable experiences as a fill-in pianist helped shape my views on worship as a whole, and church music in particular. I love Ecclesiastes 3:11, which says, *"He has made all things beautiful in its time."* It was His time, and His timetable.

My mother's prayer somehow became my own. As my children came along, my desire to see them embrace music as a way of life grew more fervent. I was intentional about playing all kinds of music in the house as they grew up, especially praise and worship and classical genres. Psalm 59:16-17 became a guiding Scripture: *"But I will sing of your power; yes I will sing aloud of your mercy in the morning; for you have been my defense and refuge."* Gradually, I was becoming more confident as a worship leader. I discovered how satisfying it was to plan and run a well-organized worship practice.

It was after my daughters started taking guitar lessons that the season of increase began. They improved so quickly, under the expert direction of an incredibly versatile and experienced teacher, so much so that they were able to join me on the platform when I was either leading or playing under another leader. Bringing guitars to summer camp and jamming with friends who play multiple instruments, suddenly brought home ideas I had been trying to impress on them for years. Ideas like, it's so much FUN to collaborate with other musicians!

This musical explosion seemed to develop very quickly. But, as I look back over the several seasons that came before, I see the hand of God laying the groundwork. During the frustration of my youth group years, when I was a little fish in a big pond of far superior musicians, the hunger was born. The years after I left home and bounced around numerous small churches where the need for musicians of any caliber was great, refined my gifting. The patient shaping of my own young kids' musical influences and tastes at times was a thankless task, yet this furthered my continued and growing passion to become a musician, a leader of worship.

Only hindsight reveals there actually WAS a process at all, and that it was God's, designed to accomplish His purpose in my life and in my kids' lives. They are all still teens – time will tell whether they choose to use their musical training to glorify God, or even "just" for their own enjoyment. My learning curve at the different stages was always steep; I keenly felt the pressure of inadequacy, and the fear of failure.

Three things I have learned over the course of 25-plus years of developing into the musician I longed to be.

1. *It's not about me.* In the early days, I was focused on glory for myself, getting up in front of people to showcase my own abilities. Thankfully, God ensured those prideful tendencies were smacked down by painful doses of reality. I began to see the bigger picture of serving God's people by being useful to the Body of Christ, using the gifts and talents He's given me.

2. *When a worship service seems to flow, it's not by accident.* My love of organization and being ultra-prepared has served me well in this regard. When the worship leader has spent time earnestly seeking God for direction, this sets the tone for the rehearsal time, and the subsequent worship service. I take Psalm 33:3

seriously: *"Sing to Him a new song; play **skillfully**, and shout for joy."*

3. *It's not a performance.* What a privilege to lead God's people in praise and worship to Him! Preparation is definitely important, but it's my attitude towards the congregation I'm serving, and the Lord we're singing about, that is paramount.

I was frustrated with my slow musical progress in my younger years. I wanted to be "good enough" right away, without putting in the work and the years of practice. Listening to and playing with other musicians is where the greatest opportunities for improvement lie, and I hope that process continues all my life.

God heard my Mother's heartfelt cry to "bring back the music". Little did she know it wasn't only for her, but for the generations that would follow.

Jennifer Johnson *is a wife, home-educating mom, music teacher and worship leader. She loves encouraging women to hear from and draw closer to her strong, loving God.*

Walking in Your Destiny living in HIS increase

Two Hearts Two Souls

Suzanne D Jubb

We all remember Forest Gump's famous words, "life is like a box of chocolates, you never know what you are going to get." For some of us it is the death of a loved one, for some it is cancer, for some it is a broken relationship, the list goes on and on. For myself, it was my husband leaving the relationship after 17 years of marriage and leaving without giving a reason why.

In October of 1999, Jim said that he no longer loved me. Wow, how do you deal with that? What do you say? How do you say it? What do you do?

My first thought was, what part of this did I miss? I love my family dearly, I work hard for my family and I do the best I can. How can this be? The world as I knew it started to break apart before my very eyes. From then on, the road became rocky. Communication was extremely difficult because everything that came out of my mouth seemed like the wrong thing to say. Tension was high.

By May of 2000, my husband volunteered at one of my events, put his arms around me and said we will be the best of friends or get married again. It was a tender moment, unexpected, and confusing to say the least.

In June he said he was leaving...and in July he left. He left without telling me where he was going. At that point, my world crumbled into bits and pieces. It was a huge challenge to keep everything together, with four kids between the tender ages of 10 to 16. Nothing made sense to me. I was broadsided.

I wasn't expecting too much at the end of the month as my birthday came along. Surprisingly, I did get a card from Jim but it wasn't your usual birthday card. The front of the card said HOPE. Inside the card he had written, "I love you and I think of you each and every day. Learn to relax and you shall find happiness." Happiness????...I WAS happy! Yes...tired, grumpy at times...yes, but unhappy? That was NOT me. Is that how Jim saw me?

Communication was at a minimum. I had to wait till he called me. The pain of not knowing where he was unbelievable. Maybe he would show up to the games. The kids were elite hockey players. First period, no Jim. Second period, no Jim. Third period he would come strolling in. This was not the Jim that I knew. The Jim that I knew was an awesome dad and good provider. He had been there 24/7 for the kids and for me. He was the man that would tell his co-workers that he could not wait to get home to see his wife and family. This was the man that had coached his children and that would call from work in the middle of a game to see how the kids were doing. This was the man that would tenderly and skillfully sit the kids at the table and talk to them when there were issues that needed to be discussed.

I thought he was having a nervous breakdown. What other explanation could there be? Being unfaithful was not even an option. After all we, had made a promise to each other the day we got married that we would never be unfaithful. That at the very least we would end the relationship before that thought even occurred. A promise is not to be taken lightly. It is something that you never break. It's your word. It's your integrity at stake. Another woman was the last thing I suspected.

When I came to the realization that he might be having a nervous breakdown, I called one of his co-workers. I was concerned. Where was Jim? Was he safe? Was he contemplating suicide? The first words that came from the co-worker was "Don't you know?" Know what? In that moment I put two and two together. In the months before he left, Jim had given me subtle hints about a co-worker named Donna. How she had worn a red dress to get his attention at one of the functions we attended and how they had met for coffee and she had given him a hug. Immediately, I asked the co-worker for Donna's number. He said he would call me back in a minute.

To my surprise, Donna was the one who called me back. She admitted to the affair but was sad because he was no longer with her. "Are you kidding me?" "Do you have any idea what you have done?" "Did you think for a minute what this might do to my children?" These were some of the questions I asked her. I ended with, "I have no respect for you" and then I got off the phone. In that instant the world as I knew it collapsed entirely.

At that point, I was at my lowest. I felt like I was one with the carpet, as low as low can go. I felt heavy, defeated, drained, with no knowledge of what my next step would be. I also remember seeing a knife on the table and thinking that twisting that knife into my heart would not even come close to the pain I was feeling. How do I get myself out of this pit of hell? Do I call a friend? Maybe later. Do I call my mom? Maybe tomorrow. What about God. Will He hear my cry or is He just someone you meet when you go to heaven? What did I have to lose and so I cried, "God, I don't like where I am at, PLEASE help me out of this mess."

That very moment, something magical happened. A stirring deep within. A connection so deep that awoke me to the realization that this must be my soul. Something I had never felt before. It was warm and loving. It was my glimmer of hope. My first step away from this nightmare.

I did not go to work that day nor the day after. I hardly ate and the only sane thing I knew to do, to handle this enormous amount of stress, was to run so I could relieve some of the pressure. With little food and running twice a day, it wasn't long before I dropped two sizes.

On my third day, I drove to work but could not make it out of the car. On the fourth day, I drove to work, made it out of the car but my legs felt like lead; every step was like the weight of pulling my boots out of mud, one step at a time. I made it to the point of starting up my computer but ended up staring at it for the remainder of the day. On the fifth day, I was ready to work but it was toilsome to focus. I prayed that I might be able to have some peace and lo and behold God covered me with a blanket of peace which miraculously gave me the ability to work. Wow! ...an answered prayer! God REALLY does hear and answer prayer!

Later, Jim left me a note. It said. "Two hearts, two souls, two people in love, what do we have, what do we want, who do we need to be."

Since that day my life has been an incredible journey of intense learning and a quest to find the answer to this question: **How can two people who love each other so much end up in such a predicament?**

You see Jim did not leave because he did not love me. I also have a better understanding of the dynamics that lead to affairs. I know that we failed miserably at communication and that listening was not one of my best skills. I truly believe that had I had the skills then that I have acquired since, Jim and I would still be together.

I have always said that if I can save one marriage from the same kind of pain of divorce which Jim and I faced, through the knowledge I have accumulated over the years, my experience will have been worth it. God has now provided me with such an opportunity.

My knowledge has increased exponentially over the years and God provided the means and the avenues. Many excursions were a leap of faith that financially it would all work out and it did.

God did help me out of this mess and I continue to hold on to His promise that ...**all things work together for good to them that love God, to them who are called according to his purpose. Romans 8:28 KJV**

You see when you invite God into your life He reveals himself to you in powerful ways. Early in my walk with God, He gave me a

Scripture. How do you know it was God, you ask? Well, when three different people give you the same scripture reference in one week, it's a God thing! My Scripture **...Trust in the Lord With all thine heart and lean not unto thine own understanding, in all thy ways acknowledge Him and He will direct thy paths. Proverbs 3: 5-7 KJV**

Not a day goes by that I don't think of that Scripture and God continues to direct my path. I am also getting better at trusting His voice. As I write this, I am at an "A Book is Never a Book Boot Camp" and there is no doubt in my mind that I need to be here. As God continues to direct my path, I know that He will not waste any of my hurts. Helping others heal their broken relationships is unfolding as my purpose. I look forward to working with God as He opens each door because with God all things are possible. To even think that I can succeed without Him as I deal with tender hearts would be foolish.

God is faithful, loving and provides me with all my needs. I challenge you to ask Him into your heart. Your life will never be the same.

Suzanne Jubb *is the author of the Golden Goose – One Important Step to Financial Freedom and soon to be released, A Journal - Questions that Really Matter. She is a speaker, a coach and passionate about teaching. Her gift is her ability to simplify the material so that all learners can benefit.*

Walking in Your Destiny
living in HIS increase

My Story Has Changed!

Margie McIntyre

I got saved shortly after I was married. However, I had to live the difficult life as the wife of an unsaved husband who belittled my newfound faith and berated me for going to church and loving God. Ten years later, he actually became a Christian, but within 2 years, our marriage ended in divorce. This was the unfortunate result of us both trusting in and being ruthlessly deceived by a "Christian" man.

That same man was a master at brainwashing, control, and manipulation. We fell for it: hook, line, and sinker! It took only three months for my husband to be tricked into believing that I no longer loved him, and one day, he just left! I was devastated, angry, hurt, and very vulnerable.

I became this "Christian" man's victim in a cult-like environment for 15 years. I was physically, sexually, spiritually, emotionally, and financially abused. I could not understand what I was doing wrong to be treated in this way.

As strange as it may sound, I thought I was where God wanted me to be. This man constantly used and twisted Scripture to keep me confused. He managed to isolate me from all of my family and friends, even my children, as he masterfully played with my mind. My loyalty to him was uncanny.

I now understand that I most likely was suffering from something called "Stockholm Syndrome". This is a condition where victims show strange and unreasonable loyalty towards their captors or abusers.

Then, one day, it was all over! Just like that! In 2003, God rescued me and moved me to another city where I found a small church that helped me to establish a proper foundation for my Christianity. I began a healing journey that brings me to today.

I moved to Red Deer in 2008 to be close to one of my sons and his family. I was so terribly afraid that they wouldn't accept me because of all the mistakes I had made, but they did.

Sadly, hurt and heartache didn't stop with escaping the influence of that one man. I thought I had healed over the last 8 years that I had been single, and I thought I was ready for a new relationship. So three years after moving to Red Deer, I married a man that I was sure I would spend the rest of my life with.

A week later, my 5-year-old grandson died unexpectedly. This tore our hearts out and devastated us all. It was a sad way for my husband and I to start our new life together.

It wasn't long before my new marriage began to show consistent signs and symptoms of major difficulties. We tried counseling and a marriage retreat, but to no avail. Meanwhile, my father died, and then my sister, my precious sister, died, and this added to the stress levels within the home. With all of these tragedies and marital problems, our short, 4-year marriage began its final decline. When I was kicked out of my home in January of last year, I realized with deep shock that I had been in yet another abusive relationship.

Yes, a number of very sad things have happened in my life. I'm not asking for sympathy. We all have a story to tell, but why was my story so full of broken and disturbing relationships?

An important truth I have learned is this: *When you don't understand the damage that has been done to your heart, you tend to repeat destructive life cycles over and over again!* This past year, I have become aware of the damage that has been done to my heart, not through physical beatings, but through the emotional and verbal abuse that was inflicted on my siblings and myself as children by our Mom.

Please understand that I loved my Mom. However, I recognize now that she was a person who was hurting. Out of her own unsolved hurts, she damaged our hearts with her unkind words and controlling behaviors. As a child, I internalized those things that were said and done to me and have held onto them in my heart for all these years. I wasn't good enough; I wasn't lovable; I could never do things well enough; I was unworthy; I wasn't smart enough; I would never be successful; and more.

Consequently, I was attracted to men who treated me the way I saw myself – with no value or worth. Finally, with help from a counselor, and hard work on my part, I have become aware of what was going on for so many years. I have answers to all the abuse I have received in my relationships. Previously, I hadn't realized it was abuse because I was used to being treated that way. My thoughts were that I was tough, and so I could take it.

The Lord has revealed many more things to me concerning my mother and all my intimate relationships, the domestic abuse that was involved, and the carnage it has left behind. My heart has been so broken as I have realized how much my children have suffered through all of those miserable years as well. I have faced some very difficult truths and have had to take responsibility for choices I've made, including abusive behaviors I have inflicted on others, due to destructive cycles being repeated. And I have suffered the consequences resulting from all of that. It has not been an easy journey! Thankfully, I know Jesus, and I know that I am forgiven!

I didn't cause the people I loved to abuse me. They made those choices for themselves, and they will have to answer for them one day. I am aware that, although I did not cause the abuse, I was trained up from early childhood to believe that I deserved poor treatment. Therefore, I consistently attracted it. Clearly, I have had to face that truth, and I have made a choice to do something about it.

Only now, with my new awareness of domestic abuse, do I finally understand what happened to me in the past and why I fell victim to these cruel men. I could have stayed stuck in all those memories. As a matter of fact, I did get stuck there for a while. Thankfully, I have loving friends – friends who care about me and want the best for me. They have challenged me, telling me I have potential, encouraging me to step out in faith and into a new chapter in my life. I do not need to stay in my old story! I can make a choice to move on, and Christ will change my story, as I trust Him to lead and guide me into a new future!

The crazy thing is that the new chapter in my life had already started while I was still stuck in my past. I was afraid...afraid to believe that things could actually be good in my life. The hurt in my heart will always be there, but I have the choice to stay stuck in the past or to move beyond it.

This past Good Friday, I made a decision. I finally acknowledged my fears were sin, and that both fear and faith cannot reside in my mind at the same time. I asked the Lord to forgive my fearfulness. I told Him I wanted to move on to a new chapter in my life, one of believing and living in faith.

A friend of mine shared a scripture with me.

1 Peter 5:10 says, *"And after you have suffered a little while, the God of all grace (Who imparts all blessing and favor), Who has called you to His own eternal glory in Christ Jesus, will Himself complete and make you what you ought to be, establish and ground you securely, and strengthen, and settle you."* (AMPC)

On Easter Sunday morning before church, the Lord gave me understanding! He made it clear that He had completed me, established me, strengthened me, and settled me…at the cross! My heart leapt at the soundness of my new revelation! I decided to choose faith and cast off fear, and the Lord met me with his mercy and truth!

A long time ago – at the cross – the Lord set me up for a new life in Him. I hadn't believed that. Yet, way back then, He set me up to overcome!

I know now that it's my responsibility to believe in the Lord's finishing work and move on in my life – in faith! The Lord had set me up for victory and success all along, and I had chosen to hang onto my fears instead of believing what He had done for me. How mistaken I have been!

In church that Easter morning, it was confirmed by my pastor's message titled "Change Your Story" that my story has been changed because of Christ!

Now I get it. When I step into the waters in faith as the Israelites did, the Lord will meet me there, and He will part the sea. Nothing is impossible for God!

I have suffered a little while. But now I know that I have been made perfect in Him. I am established, strengthened, and settled in Jesus Christ.

Why has it been such a long journey? Only God knows. However, I have no problem understanding three very specific things:

1. That God works all things together for good for those who love Him.

2. That He doesn't waste a single hurt.

3. That He has been forming me into the image of His Son all along.

I have started a new chapter in my life! My story has changed! I am living in His increase! I am free of 60 years of bondage!

This journey has been my training ground. If I haven't known what it is to hurt, I cannot truly understand someone who is hurting. I have hurt, yes, and I have felt pain to very my core. Yet, if there is someone whose heart and life can be turned toward the Lord because I can understand, help, and encourage, it is all worth it!

Margie McIntyre is the author of Mind Matters – Change Your Mind, Change Your Life and lives in Red Deer, Alberta. She is a financial coach and also a very proud mother of four children and grandmother of eight wonderful grandchildren.

Walking in Your Destiny
living in HIS increase

Anchovies, Spaghetti Squash, and a Chocolate Bar

Daniela Peregrina

There is a popular cooking competition that airs on the Food Network channel. **Chopped** is a cooking competition that challenges and mocks the culinary knowledge of four chefs, and it results in one of them winning the coveted $10,000 prize. Each chef must cook an appetizer, an entrée, and a dessert using the secret ingredients contained in the baskets placed at their cooking stations at the beginning of each round. With only 20 minutes to complete each dish, once they have managed to cook something using ALL of the secret basket ingredients, they face a panel of judges at the "Chopping Block". Needless to say, this is a competition, so one of the competitors is eliminated after each round. He or she is "chopped" from the competition.

This challenge shouldn't be difficult for a chef, right? Wrong! Each basket contains an array of proof that the producers of the show have a pretty twisted sense of humor.

What would you do if you were handed a basket that contained anchovies, spaghetti squash, and a chocolate bar in it? What if you were asked to create a restaurant-worthy dish from such mismatched ingredients?

Isn't life like that at times? We are handed a basket filled with trials and tribulations, challenges and setbacks. I have been faced many times with a basket that I thought was a joke, a ridiculous way of challenging me to break and walk away. With savory and sweet ingredients that just didn't seem like they could be used to create an edible dish, those times urged me through the invading thoughts in my mind to just shut the basket and walk away from the "cooking station". I could clearly visualize a chef looking at the anchovies, spaghetti squash, and the chocolate bar thinking, "This is just *not* possible!" I have found myself reinforcing the same words in my own mind.

But…what if, just maybe, this *could* work?

Three years ago I was challenged with a "basket" that contained bitter and unknown ingredients. I was suddenly single, left by the man I believed I was going to grow old with. My ingredients were a teenaged son, a debilitating illness from which I would never recover, unemployment, and a world of questions. Why? How? When? My brain screamed: Walk away from it ALL! YOU CAN'T DO THIS!

I began slowly to shut the basket. I felt like my world was collapsing. My "ingredients" were stronger than I was.

I live in a small town in California, the kind of town where you cannot take a trip to the grocery store to purchase milk without several cordial exchanges of, "How's the family?" and "What's new?"

Not wanting to face the inevitable questions that people I ran into would ask, or the possibility of breaking down sobbing in the cereal aisle, I became a hermit. I avoided going out. I shut my basket.

"You need to pull it together!" "Think of your son!" Friends and family would offer advice and support with the hope that my situation would change and I would suddenly snap out of it. However, that is one reality of grief; it cannot be shut off like a light switch.

One summer day, I received a call from my mother. She tried as hard as she could to be kind, but there was a commanding strength in her voice. "Baby Girl, I want you to know that God will shower you with His blessings, and He will fill your basket. So open it, and make sure it's a big one!" Although I appreciated her checking in on me and encouraging me with her words, all I could think was, "Right. Sure. Whatever!"

A few days after that, I decided to finally go out. In the high desert of the California Southern Sierras, summers are warm with gentle breezes, and it was Farmer's Market time in Tehachapi. I showered, got dressed, and prepared to go out. My 14-year-old son was away at a Boy Scout summer camp in Virginia. He was so far, and I missed him, so I would have to do this on my own.

Purse, keys, and my sunglasses were all in my hand. The pit in my stomach reminded me that this was probably not a good idea. As I walked towards the front door, I dropped my keys. I bent down to pick them up, and right there, on the threshold of my front door, a scorpion scurried right by my keys. I jumped back, screamed like a little girl, and ran back to the living room! What do I do? What on earth is that thing doing in my house? I didn't even know we had these vile creatures in our area! Frantically, I called my Dad. He would definitely know what to do!

I kept an eye on the intruder, making sure it didn't get away before I got it. "Hello, Lala!" my Dad answered in his regular, upbeat, and loving voice.

"There is a SCORPION in my house! What do I do? How do I kill it? Oh, my gosh!" I screamed into the phone, rattling off my words quicker than I ever thought I could speak. He calmed me down with his gentle words and a few questions.

Panic, fear, and helplessness all flooded my body. With my Dad still on the phone, I said with determination, "I'm doing this, and I will call you back when it's done."

I went and got a book, the biggest book I could find in my library, and tossed it from the other side of the room towards my nemesis. Missed! I went back for a second, and a third, and it kept scurrying away. And each time, I would scream.

"Dear God, please help me do this!" I uttered the words without really expecting God to help. I mean, it was only a bug, right? But at that moment, the last book I decided to toss fell...and a crunching sound followed.

Yes! I no longer was shaking. I no longer felt helpless, although I did feel bad for the creature that lied underneath the Larousse Dictionary. I was now ready to go out, and I stepped over the mountain of books spread across my foyer.

I arrived at the Farmer's Market. I parked the car and tried to get out. It was as if I had already loaded my arms with produce-filled bags, and they were weighing me down. No matter how hard I tried, I could not manage to get out of the car.

It was getting warm, and I was watching all the happy people walk by. I could hear the music playing in the park. Finally managing to get out of my car, I bowed my head as I moved slowly towards the busy market booths.

My eyes felt like they were burning. I had been crying every day for two months. Farmer's Market used to be a time of the year that brought me such joy. I have always loved to come home with fresh produce or a handmade craft or trinket...but today was different. The booths that lined the park downtown did not seem to have anything that enticed me to want to go visit them.

I mostly walked with my head down and my glasses on. "Hello, Child! What is troubling your heart?" A voice with an accent I didn't recognize called out to me and was followed by a hand on my shoulder. Stopping to raise my eyes, I was met with a kind smile from an African woman who was now holding both my shoulders.

"What troubles you? Why are you so sad?" In that moment, the floodgates burst open, and I started to sob and could not utter any words. She gently guided me to a chair inside the booth where a man sat on the ground weaving baskets. The woman then knelt down in front of me and told me to give my problems to God, that no matter how difficult I thought the time I was going through was, He would take care of it all. Only He could give my heart the peace that it needed.

Her words were kind, and they soothed me as she hugged me. The man on the floor now handed me a tissue and continued to weave his basket. As I wiped my tears, I looked up and noticed all of the beautiful baskets surrounding me. Suddenly, my mother's words echoed in my head, "Baby Girl, I want you to know that God will shower you with His blessings, and He will fill your basket. So open it, and make sure it's a big one!"

In my car, driving home with a new basket on the passenger seat, I reflected on what had happened. I now had a basket, and a prayer, but most of all, I had hope – hope that God would provide and take care of me during this time in my life.

As I walked through the front door, the pile of books I had thrown at the scorpion greeted me. One by one, I picked them up and did not feel the fear of reencountering my unwelcome houseguest. To my surprise, the scorpion was no longer there when I kicked away the book I thought had landed on it to the side. However, I didn't even worry about it.

In the living room, a warm glow was shining through the window as the sun set for the day. On the couch, a basket and my Bible were next to me. I prayed like I had never prayed before – prayers for peace, for strength, for forgiveness, and for patience.

"The Lord is good to everyone and everything; God's compassion extends to all his handiwork!" (Psalm 145:9, CEB) I knew in my heart, without any doubt, as I read the book of Psalms, that God would extend His love, blessings, and compassion to me. The next few days were filled with hope and a new feeling of purpose as I prepared for the return of my son from summer camp.

A few days after the encounter with the basket woman at the Farmer's Market, I received the first of many blessings that would fill my basket. I received a job offer – a new beginning, a breath of hope. This was only the beginning of my showers of blessings.

One by one, my basket was also filled with the fruits of the Holy Spirit. *"But the fruit of the Spirit is love, joy, peace, patience, kindness, goodness, faithfulness, gentleness and self-control. There is no law against things like this."* (Galatians 5:22-23, CEB)

As my basket was filled, the contents were not always what I expected. However, even the challenging and bitter ingredients opened my eyes to the hidden blessings that can come once they are all combined to form something good. What I once thought was a disjointed mess could be turned into something purposeful and appealing. Looking back now three years later, I can see that God put exactly what I needed into my woven vessel. His will prevailed, and my life has forever been changed.

"Your basket and your kneading bowl will be blessed. You will be blessed when you are out and about and blessed when you come back." (Deuteronomy 28:5-6, CEB)

So, now when I see anchovies, spaghetti squash, and a chocolate bar in my basket, I step back and think, "I might not know what I will cook with these ingredients, but I know God has a plan for a culinary masterpiece! It will be delectable and worthy of a five-star rating, for He is the Head Chef and will give me direction. I will no longer fear being "chopped" when I approach the chopping block."

Daniela Peregrina *is a mother, teacher, actress, playwright, director, and entrepreneur. She has co-written plays and co-owns a dinner-mystery theater company. Feeding friends and family in her kitchen in Tehachapi, California, is one of her passions. She is working on her first book, which will be published in 2017.*

Walking in Your Destiny living in HIS increase

A Strong Tower

Cheryl Regier

I grew up in a loving, Christian home. Raised in the church, it was a natural decision for me to give my life to the Lord at a very young age. Personally, *not* living a life of faith was never a consideration for me.

As part of my faith walk, I was water-baptized around age 10 or so. In the Christian community, most people understand that water baptism is a representation of the death of the old man or nature (symbolized by being submerged under water) and of the nature of Christ – the new man – coming forth or being birthed (symbolized by being raised up out of the water). When one is water-baptized, that person is making public their commitment to leave behind the old nature and to embrace the new life that is theirs in Christ.

At the time, my family was attending a charismatic church fellowship. It was common practice after each person was raised up out of the water for people within the congregation, if led by the Lord, to share a prophetic word for that particular individual. That day, the Lord gave me a very specific and impactful word that declared that I would "be a strong tower in a chaotic time".

That's a pretty powerful word when you meditate on it! As a young child, not yet a teenager, the impact of that word didn't register at all. For me, life continued on in the same way as before. Working towards being a "strong tower" did not factor into any of my personal decisions at that time.

Here's an important point to remember, though. I have heard it preached that God gives prophetic words about people's future to reveal to them the desire and the outcome that He has planned for their life...their destiny calling. Although God loves and accepts us in the now, as we are with all of our imperfections, He also loves us enough to want to transform us into who He sees us becoming in the future.

Prophecy serves to show us God's intention for our lives. Obviously, then, prophetic words aren't realized and fulfilled until later. In the meantime, each person with a God-given word over his or her life is in process. This process is defined by growth, especially in the spiritual sense. In order to see that word fulfilled, there needs to be a "growing up in God" that allows the individual to travel from where they are in the present to that place of where they become who God has called them to be.

By its very nature, what is spoken over us in prophecy speaks to who we are not _yet_. Prophesy demands that we enter into a period of development that allows those words to be realized and perfected in us. Our character must to go through a transformation that will permit us to walk in that calling successfully. Our development will include experiences that impart knowledge and wisdom that, in turn, gives us the authority and authenticity to live out that word.

God declares to us in Scripture: *So shall My word be that goes forth from My mouth; It shall not return to Me void, but it shall accomplish what I please, and it shall prosper in the thing for which I sent it.* (Isaiah 55:11, NKJV)

This verse reminds us of the power in God's spoken word. From His perspective, He will do everything in His power to see it manifest in a person's life. When we cooperate with God – aligning ourselves up with His intention for us through our agreement and our subsequent actions – we can affect the timelines of that word and its fulfillment. On the flip side, if we are in disobedience, we can delay what God intends for our life, affecting our development. Finally, there are words that must go through a very particular period of germination and growth before they come to fruition. These words are dependent on certain times, seasons, people, and events. For one to operate in that new place of fulfillment, other things must first be established or be present in order to do so.

As it is said in Habbakuk 2:3: *For the vision is yet for an appointed time; But at the end it will speak, and it will not lie. Though it tarries, wait for it; Because it will surely come, it will not tarry.* (NKJV)

There is an appointed time set for the prophetic words that are spoken over our lives. The word of God over me at my baptism spoke of such a time. For me, to be a strong person was not necessarily the issue. I tend to be strong-willed as it is, and I am very firm and assertive in my convictions and beliefs. However, I needed to have built up on the inside of me the spiritual and character strength that could withstand the chaos of a time when others would falter. I could not be in a place of operating out of my own human strength and power. Instead, my development had to be at a point when the word would accomplish God's will and intent for my life and for His kingdom purposes. Growth and maturity needed to be present. The manifestation of the increase God had for me also depended on a season of turbulence and chaos. My rising up had an appointed time.

I have found myself reflecting on this word over my life in recent months and years. God has reminded me of it on more than one occasion. In looking back at what God has done in my life and developed within me, I can see where I have risen up in my anointing and calling to be that strong tower during chaotic times. He has been showing me that I *have* been operating in that "strong tower" anointing throughout my life in various degrees. Even when I was not aware of it, His intention for my life was being demonstrated during times of struggle and turmoil.

Throughout my life, the evidence of my prophetic word has been shown in many ways. I have made decisions that have conflicted with societal norms. I have had to be strong and authentic in my beliefs in a time when pressure from the outside would have me compromise. I have passions and convictions that have required God's strength to uphold and be true to. Called also to be a "ministry of helps" to people, I have used my gift for words and practical helps to encourage and build up others. This encouragement has been born out of the fire of tough times and experiences and out of the revelations that God has brought into my life. My family and I have experienced some serious situations, particularly a bad business deal that affected my husband's job and our family's security and future. I have been a strong tower for my husband during a time of great turmoil and setback, standing by him in support and encouragement when perhaps others in similar situations would have quit and left. During a historical time of secularism and attacks on Christian values and morals, I am rising up as a watchman on the wall, taking a stand for what is right. I *am* living my destiny calling.

With these recent reminders of the anointing God has given me, I am also being challenged in my present to embrace a deeper understanding of what this word means for me in my life moving forward. I know that I am being asked to upgrade and increase my capacity for this word to operate through me in a greater way. In addition, I know that my experiences in the past have been "trial runs" so to speak. As I've grown up in God, I have had opportunities to practice what He has declared over my life. Each experience that I have had prepares me for the future and the increase that God has waiting for me within my anointing.

This challenge obviously involves a faith upgrade. I can't think and be as I was in the past if I am going see an increase in my ability to be a strong tower during chaotic times. Growth and maturity will be prerequisites to seeing the enlargement of this word in my life.

I am sensing the Holy Spirit's prompting to embrace this upgrade. This comes with the knowledge and understanding that it will only be by God's grace that I will be enabled to grow up in my calling. I know that sacrifice and trials will be a part of this journey. That can be scary at times, but I have to remind myself that fear and faith cannot co-exist. If I am going to accept my responsibility of development, I cannot give in to the spirit of fear. On the other hand, it is also an exciting time. As I meditate on the possibilities of God, I am encouraged to look forward to what He has in store for me as a result of His promised increase in my life.

We are definitely living in uncertain times. Many people are going through extremely difficult, horrible, even tragic circumstances. If I am going to cooperate with God working through me to be a source of strength during these chaotic times, I absolutely have to live in His increase in ever expanding fullness.

Three things I have learned as I reflect on this specific word God has spoken into my life:

1. *God's intention for our lives doesn't change.* His desire to see His purpose for our lives fulfilled doesn't waver. We must cooperate with Him to see it manifest, knowing that He can perfect it in us over time and through process. In addition, we need to reflect back once in a while, looking at our past through God's lens, in order to see how He has been true to His word in our lives. If we are still waiting for our promise from

God to come to fruition – our increase – reviewing our life's experiences through God's eyes will help us to recognize the training and preparation He is graciously giving us so that we can be ready to fully receive in the future.

2. *God's word waits for the appointed time.* My prophetic word came to me as a young child, but did not start manifesting until I was an adult. The evidence of my anointing has become increasingly more apparent in the last decade or more. Patience and perseverance is necessary for the journey.

3. *God is not content with good enough.* His plans for our lives involve enlargement and an expansion of our territory. What I have gone through by God's grace in the past has enabled me to operate in my anointing in ever increasing fullness. It is training me for a much larger platform of what God is doing and desires to do on a greater scale.

These lessons apply to everyone. God's intention for you and your destiny calling have not changed. It awaits an appointed time. In addition, He is not content to leave you in a place of restriction, but wants to enlarge you as you move forward in your faith walk with Him.

Cooperate with God.

Be patient and persevere in your faith.

Look to the future and an expansion of your territory.

Be a strong tower in *your* calling for God's glory and His kingdom purposes!

Cheryl Regier is married to a wonderful husband and is the mother to six amazing sons. She works from home as a writer and editor in addition to homeschooling. She loves to serve people through imparting encouraging words, practical helps, and meaningful gifts.

Walking in Your Destiny living in HIS increase

Birth of BACC
(Bibles at Cost Canada)

Karen Skelton

Conception began while I was in my mid-fifties.

Our children were pretty much launched; my husband John was well established in his corporate career and for the first time in my life I was faced with thinking about the "empty nest" soon to manifest. As I contemplated the coming years, I began to pray about how God would want me to fill them. I asked Him to give me "something" that would <u>hold my interest for the rest of my life</u>; "something" that would <u>matter for all of eternity</u>! Later, I added another qualifier to this prayer saying, "God it would really be good if You could give me something that would <u>make me a lot of money</u> too! That way I could help pay off our mortgage; and then John wouldn't mind if I give money away." Through my home church I would occasionally hear of special projects towards which I always wanted to donate but I knew that my husband, generous though he is, would not be happy with me if I started giving away chunks of my income.

During the time I consider to be the first trimester of this "pregnancy", I accepted a variety of temp assignments through one of the local downtown agencies. Between assignments, I volunteered sporadically at my home church and eventually accepted a position as Administrative Assistant to one of our pastors.

My second trimester began when one day, "my" pastor asked me if I could please find "those little Bibles" that we give away to new believers. When I went looking for them, I found that our source had dried up and those "little Bibles" were no longer available. My instruction was to find Bibles that are "very good and very cheap". Tall order!

Canadian Bible Society seemed like a good place to begin my search. There I discovered a New Testament that was absolutely perfect. It had forty pages of question and answer instructions to help a new believer navigate the passages that would begin to establish understanding of salvation and discipleship. Problem was that it was too expensive. The price tag was seven dollars and forty cents per Bible - this in the year 2000! (At today's cost, they would very likely be double that amount!) For the purposes of our outreach, the Bibles needed to be purchased in case lots and our budget simply did not accommodate the expense.

I identified that the Bible was published at Tyndale House in Chicago so, naively, I thought perhaps this large, well-known publisher might give me a more affordable price. No one there was willing even to speak with me.

Now on a mission, I searched the internet, landing on a site in California and to my great surprise and excitement – there was my prized little Bible priced at 1.79 USD!! I couldn't imagine how this company was able to offer it at such a discount. The company president, Gordie Blackwell, friendly as a puppy dog as well as very knowledgeable and experienced, explained how they were able to do it. I ordered a couple of cases for our church here in Calgary to the delight of our pastors. We had opportunity to give them all away and within a couple of months I ordered two more boxes, and again, a while later I ordered even more.

Ironically, the third trimester coincided with the third time I ordered more Bibles. Gordie and I chatted a while and just as we were about to end our conversation, he said to me, "How would you like to distribute for me in

Canada?" He went on to explain that although he had some customers in Canada he really hadn't established a clientele here and the cross-border sales proved to be cumbersome. He thought it might be better to establish a Canadian office. My immediate response was, "Oh Gordie – that sounds so interesting but I wouldn't have a clue how to go about something like that. But, I go to a big church – I'll ask around and maybe I can find someone that would be interested."

A couple of days later, as I was sitting in the bathtub, the Lord spoke to me! He said, "What did you just turn down!??" His voice was like a thunderbolt and so clear to me it was as though He was sitting beside me on the edge of the tub! A flood of understanding – and fear - swept through my whole body. Understanding – that putting Bibles into people's hands would "matter for all of eternity" just as I had prayed. Fear – that I wouldn't have the slightest idea of how to set up a company. This offer was not small. The intention was that I would distribute throughout all of Canada! And more fear......knowing that this was really God speaking to me and I couldn't refuse what had been offered to me. I knew also that if I didn't respond immediately, I would talk myself out of it!

I climbed out of the tub – dripping wet – wrapped a towel around myself and went downstairs to call Gordie in California. He answered the telephone immediately and I said, "Gordie, I'm going to do it!" I told him that I didn't have any money to purchase inventory. He said, "No problem, I'll just start sending the Bibles and you start selling. You can pay me as the money comes in." My next question to Gordie was, "Do you need references?" He said "No, I don't need references – I have the Holy Spirit – and you are the right person to do this!"

A couple of days later I had a long conversation with my husband, John. who is a very wise, very experienced, very practical businessman. When I told him what I was planning to do, I could tell by his demeanor that he was less than enthusiastic, although he didn't want to hurt my feelings. I had mentioned to him that the first thing I needed was an accounting program to be installed on my computer. He suggested that I simply use a spread sheet to begin with. When I asked him why, he responded that it would be best not to spend the money until I could be sure that the business would flourish. He went on to explain to me that statistically, a large majority of new businesses fail within the first year.

My reaction to this was, "WELL!, this one will NOT FAIL! This one was given to me by the Lord and it will not fail!"

It took only two years to get into a position where I could order inventory and pay upfront!!

The faithfulness of God astounds me as I look back over the past sixteen years:

"God, please give me something that will hold my interest for the rest of my life." *I still love what I am doing.*

"God, please give me something meaningful – something that will bear fruit for all of eternity". *Only heaven will reveal how many lives have been redeemed because of this Bible Ministry*

"Oh, by the way, God, please make it something that will make me some real money." *There has never been any financial stress surrounding this business.*

As it turned out, the "lots of money part" was not necessary. A couple of months after Bibles at Cost Canada became fully and officially established, my husband came home from work one day and said casually to me,

"I did something today"

"What did you do?" I asked, thinking that maybe he had gone shopping or some other newsworthy thing that he was not in the habit of doing.

"I sold some shares and payed off the mortgage. We are completely debt free." There was no longer any need for me to help with the mortgage!

All of the answers to these requests, so casually but earnestly spoken, can be summed up in the following passages:

<u>Ephesians 3: 20, 21</u> "Now to Him who is able to do far more abundantly beyond all that we ask or think according to the power that works within us, To Him be the glory in the church and in Christ Jesus to all generations forever and ever . Amen"

<u>Philippians 4:19</u> "And My God will supply all of your needs according to His riches in glory in Christ Jesus"

The lessons learned so far throughout this journey have been many. Perhaps most surprising and impactful would be the idea that there is no such thing as a casual conversation with God. He bends low and hears every word – every thought – and He never sleeps – He's never inattentive. Most, if not all of the prayers surrounding the requests about my "empty nest" concerns were never "full-out", "on-my-face", "crying-out-to-God" kind of praying. These were more in the nature of casual conversation with God. Maybe something like a conversation one might have along the way during a walk in the park with a friend.

The second lesson unfolded along the way. I continue to be amazed at the numbers of quality people with the expertise necessary to help me learn and grow. I would have been afraid to start if I had realized how much I didn't know.

Third lesson: With God, nothing is impossible!

My "empty nest" prayer was fully answered: the infant Bibles At Cost Canada was born and today as I write this sixteen years later, Bibles At Cost Canada is still growing and maturing.

Karen Skelton is married, the mother of three beautiful daughters and grandmother of nine. She is owner of Bibles At Cost Canada which is a Bible Distribution Company supplying Bibles to churches throughout Canada.

Walking in Your Destiny
living in HIS increase

Increase – God's Step-By-Step Plan

Dannielle Somerville

I was so excited to get my first job after high school. The fact that a pet store would hire me right away was something that most kids my age only dreamt about. I had always wanted to work with animals, and it felt so good to know that I could make a difference by doing what I loved.

I enjoyed 2 years of working alongside God at that job, but I eventually knew it was time for a change. I knew that letting go of a 'for sure' thing (financially) would be a bit scary. However, I trusted that God was asking me to let go of this so that I could do something greater.

Shortly afterwards, God showed up, and I got another job at a specialized gift shop. Along with pets, gift giving is also right up my alley. I love to share sentiments with my family and friends! This is how I knew that God had His hand on me and was guiding me to the next step in my journey.

This job helped me grow in so many ways. Eventually, I worked my way up, and when one of the managers quit, I was next in line to take over the position. Within 3 months, I became a key holder, and in 8 months, a manager.

The quandary I found myself in was the fact that the company didn't have anyone to train me. It was only me and the Holy Spirit – and that is how I become a qualified manager.

It was very hard and exhausting but, at the same time, very rewarding. I loved directing a team and being in charge of setting schedules. God was doing something in my life, but I was unsure of what that was.

Once I got married, my husband and I moved to another city. This meant that again, I wouldn't have a job. I would have to trust God to help me find one that was right for me.

To make a longer story shorter, I had a taste of being a manager. Taking another retail job just didn't hold the passion or excitement for me. I knew it was time to start my own business.

Even though I could see God always had His eyes on me, I was terrified to strike out on my own. I felt stressed out because we needed two incomes to support our household. At this point, I didn't even know what I would do let alone how to do it.

That was when I started an Avon business to get into something – anything to get started and get some knowledge under my belt. I knew in my spirit that God wanted me to do a business, so that is exactly what I decided I would do. With my wonderful husband's blessing, I began my entrepreneurial journey.

After a while, I realized that this was not where God wanted me to be. I think I had gotten ahead of Him because I was pushing forward to get going. This business was not going to help support us, and it looked like I had failed. I knew I would be forced to go back to work because I couldn't make it on my own.

At that point, I felt frustrated, confused, and very, very alone. I had so much fear! I began to worry about everything. I felt like God wasn't helping me, and I began to feel resentment and rebellion towards Him. I felt myself pulling away.

I decided to do my 'own thing' and ended up getting a job. Yes, you guessed it – a retail job. I KNEW I wasn't called into retail, but I felt, again, that I needed to do something.

How did doing it my way work out for me? UGH... I was miserable! My health deteriorated, and I was constantly dealing with back pains. I even started to get migraines. At this point, I knew I needed to go back to school to pursue something that would help me become who God had called me to be.

My Mom and I prayed about my situation. I surrendered my life to God again. Right after that, He blessed me with an online university opportunity AND a way to secure every course I wanted to get at a really great price. I could actually afford to go back to school. Then, my Mom and Dad told me that they had set aside some money for my education. I didn't know that! It was a great surprise!

I began to do school and work at the same time. It was a full load, but something happened in the process. I began to be happy again.

Obviously, God was leading me to and through this. The 2 courses that were supposed to take me 6 months online only took me a week. I KNEW, once again, that it had been the right thing to do. I had starting walking in my destiny.

What I learned through this entire process is the fact that:

1. Don't try and make your own plans. Push in to God, not away.

2. Getting an education in doing what you love will make you happy.

3. Don't let fear of losing financial stability stop you from doing what God has called you to do.

The scripture that brought me to my business and through challenges that face me in business is found in Jeremiah 29:11: *"For I know the plans I have for you," declares the Lord, "plans to prosper you and not to harm you, plans to give you hope and a future."* (MSG)

When I look back at my life, I see that God has taken me step-by-step and brought increase in my life. He increased my skill set, my relationships, and my business. By trusting God as my source, instead of taking another job, He did, in fact, guide me to start my business, Proverbs 31 Events, specializing in Corporate Events and Party

Planning. Because I am exactly where He wants me in life, my business has made money every single month since its conception.

That is the blessing of walking in my destiny and living in His increase.

Dannielle Somerville *lives with her husband, Leon, in Red Deer, Alberta. She is a Pet Mom of Shyloh (Bassador) and Skittles (Rag Doll cat). She is an Author and the Founder of Proverbs 31 Events.*

Walking in Your Destiny
living in HIS increase

The Jesus I Never Knew

Deborah Hoback Veuger

It was a gloomy October afternoon, 2006, in a small rural Saskatchewan hospital. I would rather have been anywhere else in the world than here. Not because I was sitting at the bedside of my mother, but because she was dying and my heart was broken.

My mother had been diagnosed with cancer, this incredulous news leaving us in shock and disbelief. She was aghast as we were. What had started out as a stomach pain over the spring of 2004, had turned into a stage four cancer diagnosis by September of that same year. Surgery was scheduled and performed after which we were hopeful all of the cancer had been removed. Rounds of chemotherapy caused her to be very sick and yet she remained firm in her faith that God would heal and we believed right along with her. She was determined to beat this disease. I remember flying into Saskatoon, being met by my dad and my sister at the airport on our way to the University Hospital to connect with my mom. I wondered if she wanted me to stay with her and as if she read my mind, she asked if I would stay with her for this IV treatment of Chemo. I sat beside her and we smiled at each other knowing that this wasn't going to be easy but regardless, Jesus would be with her, and with us. Mom told me the story that after her first surgery, when she had returned to her hospital room, that she saw Jesus sitting in a chair watching her. At first she was very frightened, and wondered if He had come for her, but then a peace washed over her and she fell into an uncomfortable sleep. She was in excruciating pain and remembered asking Jesus to help her.

The day came when the doctors assured us that the treatments had worked and mom was in remission. We were ecstatic and praising God. Mom, we believed was healed.

As seasons passed and summer came, mom and dad took the trip to Sweden that they had always dreamed of. They enjoyed the weeks they were there but just as they were getting ready to return to Canada, mom collapsed at the airport and was admitted to a Swedish hospital. It was here that mom was told the dreaded news; the cancer had returned. On returning to Canada, more chemo treatments were prescribed and life once again was filled with everything cancer related and cancer treatment.

My mother had a great faith in Jesus and believed that He would heal her. I did too. I prayed for my mom and many of our friends and family were praying too. My mother had a wonderful church community and many blessed her with cards, gifts of food, and showed the practical loving strength of a rural Saskatchewan farm community. But as time went on, it was soon realized that without a miracle, her healing would be Eternal not earthly. My heart was in denial and I prayed fervently.

I still believed that God could do a miracle but was deeply disappointed that nothing was changing. As chemotherapy came to an end, Home Care came and went in and out of mom and dad's home, administering their compassionate hospice care; meanwhile we watched mom physically become a shell of her former self. The day came when she was admitted into our local rural hospital.

My husband and I now sat by her bedside, each lost in our own thoughts, careful that we didn't say anything that could suggest the obvious and yet each knowing what the other was thinking. Prompted by the Holy Spirit I read her favorite psalm to her again and again; Psalm 103. As I read, I continued praying that she heard it, wondered if it brought her comfort, and what she comprehended. As I finished the Psalm once again, the room grew quiet. Again we got lost in our own thoughts, feelings and reflections of what God was saying and yet too tired to really understand the meaning of the message, honestly not sure if there was one.

As I studied the scuff marks on the well worn linoleum floor, I dared to wonder what's next, not *if* but *when* she dies.... What then? I had never lost anyone close to me and I wasn't sure my heart could take it.

Something stirred in the room, and I looked up to see what was happening. A beautiful light filled the room and warmth seemed to envelope the room. We both sensed that something was different. It was a glorious presence and joy as love filled the room. It was in those moments, I turned to mom and watched her sit up in her bed. I was mesmerized by her, she looked toward the end of the bed and began a conversation with someone. She was fully aware, fully awake and her face was radiant. She smiled and her expressions were that of pure joy, as if she was greeting a long lost friend whom she deeply loved. We both heard her engage in a conversation, answering questions with great enthusiasm and anticipation. "Yes, Yes, Yes, I'm ready, Okay, yup, I'm good." In those brief moments, we both knew that my mom was having a conversation with God and in our presence we witnessed an intimate moment between our Heavenly Father and His daughter. She laid back down in her hospital bed and once more was unresponsive to my dialogue with her. She did not response to my calling out to her and not a single word was spoken.

The room was still filled with His presence and I realized in that instant that God wanted us to be a witness to the revelation of His Spirit. I had just encountered a part of Jesus that I had never known. My Spirit was alive and I felt renewed. Something changed for me. Something had increased in me and I knew that my knowledge and faith in Jesus was forever changed.

There are many lessons that God has taught me in the ten years since my mom made her journey into her heavenly home, but I will share with you three revelations that God made real for me.

1. That while we are here, we need to live out our life for God's glory and to live it to the fullest as He directs our steps. God's word became alive for me. Jeremiah 29:11 reminding me that "I know the thoughts that I think towards you; says the Lord, thoughts of peace, and not of evil; to give you a future and a hope." What I realized that day was that God was giving my mother hope and assuring her of her final home; Heaven. I had only seen it from an earthly perspective but He was making Himself real from an eternal perspective. I knew and took comfort that heaven was ours as children of God; I delighted in the knowledge that this life is not the end - it's only the beginning.

2. While we are on this journey, God will go ahead of us and lead us. His word says in Isaiah 42: 16 "I will lead them in paths that they have not known. I will make darkness light before them. And crooked places straight. These things I will do for them, and not forsake them."

3. With all that we had encountered that day, I began a new quest to know Jesus. Up to this point I knew that my relationship was solid

with Him and I felt that our communion was both sweet and deep. But I wanted to know Him more. I started to study the life of Jesus which led me to study the Feasts of the Tabernacles. I wanted to know everything about this man including His Jewish heritage. I also read and studied a book by Max Lucado called "Come Thirsty". I literally wore out the pages of the book as each reading brought a new and different revelation as to who Christ is and was. My faith deepened and strengthened as God made Himself real to me. In searching to know Him, my heart was solidified in the knowing that Jesus really was who He said and I fell in love again and again, as I discovered this Jesus I never Knew.

Deborah Veuger is married and together with her husband they have 6 amazing adult children and 7 wonderful grandchildren. She has her Masters in Christian Counseling and Education and is currently working at an agency as a therapist in Domestic Violence.

Walking in Your Destiny

living in HIS increase

God, What is YOUR Purpose for Me?

Ruth Yesmaniski

"For I know the plans I have for you," declares the LORD, *"plans to prosper you and not to harm you, plans to give you hope and a future."* Jeremiah 29:11 (NIV)

As the years pass in my life (all too quickly, I might add!), I oftentimes reflect on what effect my life has had for the kingdom of

God to this point. I continually ask, "Lord, how can I make a greater impact for Your Glory?"

Most of the time, I am convinced that God has not even started with me. It feels like the answer eludes me, no matter the number of prayers lifted to Him, the hours spent weeping before Him, the prayers before falling asleep petitioning for an answer in my dreams, the asking for Him to "speak" to me audibly or in my spirit man, or the asking for revelation through a portion of Scripture. Is there really a hope and a future for me?

After the passing of my second husband in 2011, I was subsequently challenged by Francis Chan at a Breakforth Conference in January 2012 to live out a radical love for God. After reading his book entitled *Crazy Love*, it has been my prayer to have a more committed life for God, living it out in a way that honors Him. That prayer has come to mind many times over the last three years due to the nature of some of the challenges that I have faced.

By the time the New Year's bells rang in the year 2014, I had been transplanted into a new church after 19 years of attending and serving in another one. As I began meeting new people in my new environment, I was connected with a deacon who had a unique request. I believe it was because I am a Canadian in a colored majority. This deacon approached me and asked if I would be interested in editing a book for him. I am convinced this was Divine appointment number one in revealing God's "plans to give me a hope and a future".

God knows my passion for the English language. He knows how I once taught English to a group of adults in a night class in Switzerland and what pleasure that had given me. He knows how I had wanted to become an English teacher on my return after a year off from high school, but was unable to accomplish that dream. Because I am also an immigrant to Canada, I believe I was more interested in English as a language than the majority of my peers. In addition, I have always had the "eyes" to see errors in books that I have read to the point of actually inking the changes within the book! The thought had crossed my mind many times, "I should find out how to become an editor", however, I was always too busy with a 9 to 5 job, children, marriage, church commitments, and life commitments to do so.

Yet, now, here was an open door to pursue something that I had pondered for a very long time. I agreed to edit for the deacon, and soon enough, his book was edited by the deadline. I was then asked to edit by a pastor who had a book that he wanted to publish as well. Again, I was pleased to do it.

After these two projects, the assignments came to a standstill, and I wasn't clear about the reason. After a few months, I decided I would try to advertise, first on a local website that is a center for items for sale as well as for services. I met with a couple of people, but soon found this was not the avenue I could proceed with as the content of the books were not something I would want my name associated with. It was a hard lesson to learn about the wickedness of man and the conception by those persons that their compositions would be viable literature in the mainstream of readers. Eventually, though, I was rewarded with a student who needed his resume written for a job application. By the time we were done, he was very thankful, and it was my first paying editing job!!!

Around this time, I also became heavily involved with an award show whose aim is to recognize individuals who have made a difference in other peoples' lives by their selfless acts or by empowering and encouraging others to give of themselves. The show honors everyday heroes who have done extraordinary things! The event took place in October 2015. It was a gala event attended by a record number of people, more than we had anticipated, and it was very well received.

One of the later nominations, and subsequent recipients, was a charismatic woman named Kathleen Mailer. She's a woman who is filled with the Holy Spirit's anointing, and whose ministry, among other things, is to empower women to start their own businesses and tell their own stories.

Although I did not meet her before the event, as I was more involved in the administrative duties, I was hoping to connect with her before the end of the evening, maybe even to get some advice from her as to how to proceed with this newfound interest of editing. As God would have it (not luck as some would give credit to), I was actually at the door of the banquet room as she and her husband were leaving. I introduced myself, and we started talking. As Kathleen later relayed to me, I told her I was an editor. For the life of me, though, I do not recall saying it, as I never considered myself to be so confident as to actually present myself as such, especially given the limited scope of my experience! Little did I know that she had been praying that very day for someone to come alongside of her in her business to take over a position that had just opened up…for an editor! She left, giving me her card, and saying, "We need to talk!"

I can say that I know God is faithful, but these encounters lifted me to new heights. In the midst of adverse circumstances, they have provided the ability to carry me through to a new level of faith.

I have learned through this experience, as I believed then and have had confirmed, that God is NOT finished with me yet. He DOES have a plan and a purpose for me, to give me a hope and a future that I cannot even imagine.

I have also learned that He gives us what we need, or what He wants us to experience, when He has put everything in place. He knows the number of our days. He knows what the tapestry of our life looks like – that we must be patient and allow Him to weave it.

Most importantly, I have learned that I cannot do things on my own. I have committed myself to Him, and I must lay myself aside and allow Him to live in and through me, for that is the place of true fulfilment. I cannot question Him, because He knows best what He wants to accomplish through and in my life. I can do nothing but surrender myself to Him and watch HIS GLORY be reflected in me.

Ruth Yesmaniski *is the proud mother of 4 adult sons and 8 grandchildren. She is employed in the accounting field, acting vice president of Vigor Awards International, and is also engaged in editing. Her passion is to be involved in supporting and providing hands-on service to orphans and widows around the world.*

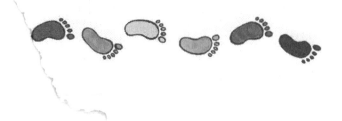

Made in the USA
San Bernardino, CA
03 May 2016